Look at the picture.
Fill the gaps using the words from the box.

| dirty | frilly | chilly | smelly | sleepy | rusty | happy | cloudy |

1 a _____ man

2 a _____ cat

3 a _____ sky

4 a _____ dog

5 a _____ bin

6 a _____ skirt

7 a _____ girl

8 a _____ bike

ar

c**ar**

Focus

Write the words with the pictures.

car	scar	farm	scarf	cart	harp
card	jar	arm	dark	park	bark

1 _____

2 _____

3 _____

Happy Birthday

4 _____

5 _____

6 _____

7 _____

8 _____

9 _____

10 _____

11 _____

12 _____

Read the words aloud.
Circle the rhyming words.

1 bar   car   ark   jar

2 dark   part   mark   bark

3 star   arm   farm   harm

4 bard   start   dart   art

5 card   hard   yard   farm

6 barn   hard   yarn   darn

7 harp   carp   sharp   shark

8 star   scar   farm   far

oi oy

c**oi**n   t**oy**

Focus

Write the words with the pictures.

voice	toy	oil	soil	boy	boil
point	coin	noise	joint	joy	coil

Key Words

oil
boil
soil

coin
join
joint
point

choice
voice

boy
joy
toy

1 _____

2 _____

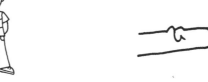

3 _____

4 _____

5 _____

6 _____

7 _____

8 _____

9 _____

10 _____

11 _____

12 _____

Extra

Fill in the missing word.

1 boil or soil

The kettle began to _____.

2 join or joint

I _____ hands with my sister.

3 voice or choice

I can hear Mrs Jones's loud _____!

4 joint or point

_____ to your sister, Anil.

5 boy or toy

My _____ is broken.

6 coin or join

I found a _____.

7 noise or moist

The dogs make a lot of _____.

8 joy or boy

What a lovely baby _____!

ear
ea

ear

h**ea**d

Focus

Write a key word to match each picture.

1 _____

2 _____

3 _____

4 _____

5 _____

6 _____

7 _____

8 _____

9 _____

Colour the letters that make the words.
Copy the new word.

1 | s | t | e | a | r |

_____ tear _____

2 | h | e | a | d | r | o |

_____

3 | n | s | p | r | e | a | d |

_____

4 | m | e | a | r | d | y |

_____

5 | b | e | a | r | d | u | m |

_____

6 | d | e | y | e | a | r |

_____

7 | s | c | l | e | a | r | b |

_____

8 | f | b | r | e | a | d | i |

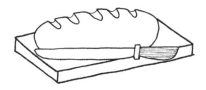

_____

er ir ur

flow**er**

b**ir**d

n**ur**se

Focus

Write the words with the pictures.

fur	skirt	kerb	shirt	hurt	herd
flower	bird	burst	stir	letter	nurse

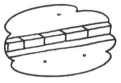

1 _____

2 _____

3 _____

4 _____

5 _____

6 _____

7 _____

8 _____

9 _____

10 _____

11 _____

12 _____

Extra

Write the words next to the things you can see in the picture.

bird   flower   herd   hurt   kerb   nurse   shirt   skirt

ou ow

mouse

cow

Focus

Write the words with the pictures.

scout	mouse	house	shout	cloud	mouth
cow	clown	owl	growl	crown	crowd

1 _____ 2 _____ 3 _____

4 _____ 5 _____ 6 _____

7 _____ 8 _____ 9 _____

10 _____ 11 _____ 12 _____

Draw a line to the rhyming word and write the word.

1  brow   shout

_____   _____

2  scout   frown

_____   _____

3  clown   cow

_____   _____

4  loud   mouth

_____   _____

5 house   cloud

_____   _____

6  south   mouse

_____   _____

or ore
aw au

h**or**se

s**ore**

y**aw**n

Focus

Write the words with the pictures.

cork	short	horn	horse	sore	snore
shore	claw	saw	crawl	paw	dinosaur

Key Words

cork
horn
fort
short
horse

more
sore

saw
claw
draw
thaw
yawn
crawl

dinosaur

1 _____

2 _____

3 _____

4 _____

5 _____

6 _____

7 _____

8 _____

9 _____

10 _____

11 _____

12 _____

Extra

Fill in the missing word.

1 stork or fork

My _____ fell on the floor.

2 torch or north

I use my _____ to read at night.

3 saw or paw

I _____ my grandma.

4 claw or straw

My lamb sleeps on _____.

5 snore or shore

My dad has a loud _____.

6 sore or more

I eat _____ chips than Mum!

7 storm or horn

The car beeped its _____.

8 astronauts or dinosaurs

I love _____.

air
ear
are

ch**air**

p**ear**

sc**are**

Focus

Write the words with the pictures.

fair	hair	chair	stairs	bear	pear
wear	tear	dare	care	scare	hare

1 _____

2 _____

3 _____

4 _____

5 _____

6 _____

7 _____

8 _____

9 _____

10 _____

11 _____

12 _____

Which word?

Copy the word to match the picture.
Colour the picture.

bare
care
hare

_____hare_____

hair
pair
air

_____

spare
stare
scare

_____

chair
stair
hair

_____

bear
pear
wear

_____

mare
dare
care

_____

airport
funfair
upstairs

_____

aircraft
airport
airway

_____

oo

b**oo**k

Focus

Write a key word to match each picture.

Key Words

book
cook
hook
look

crook
shook

foot
soot

good
hood
wood
stood

1 _____   2 _____   3 _____

4 _____   5 _____   6 _____

7 _____   8 _____   9 _____

10 _____   11 _____   12 _____

Read the words aloud.
Circle the rhyming words.

1 book   cook   look   soot

2 good   wood   foot   hood

3 pool   book   tool   fool

4 room   boot   shoot   hoot

5 goose   moose   spoon   loose

6 hoop   noon   loop   scoop

7 room   broom   groom   mood

8 crook   scar   shook   brook

days of the week

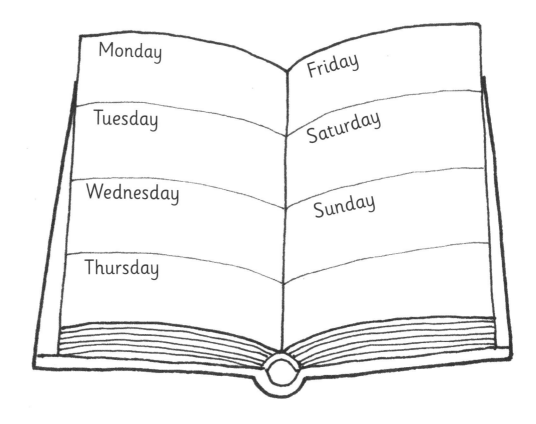

Monday
Tuesday
Wednesday
Thursday
Friday
Saturday
Sunday

Monday
Tuesday
Wednesday
Thursday
Friday
Saturday
Sunday

Focus

Write the day of the week that comes after each of these days.

1 Friday _____

2 Saturday _____

3 Tuesday _____

4 Thursday _____

5 Sunday _____

6 Wednesday _____

7 Monday _____

Read what Jess did on Monday and Tuesday.

On Monday I went to Aimee's to play.
On Tuesday I went to dance club.

Write something that happened to you on each day of the week.

On ___Monday___ I _____

_____.

On _____ I _____

_____.

On _____ I _____

_____.

On _____ I _____

_____.

On _____ I _____

_____.

On _____ I _____

_____.

On _____ I _____

compound words syllables

football

netball

Focus

Write a key word to match each picture.

Key Words

football
netball

bedroom
playroom
playground

toothbrush
toothache
toothpaste

outside
inside

airport
farmyard

1 _____

2 _____

3 _____

4 _____

5 _____

6 _____

7 _____

8 _____

Use the words in the boxes to finish the compound words.

1 | bird   berries

black _____

2 | show   port

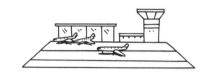

air _____

3 | dream   light

day _____

4 | top   spoon

table _____

5 | mother   children

grand _____

6 | cup   time

tea _____

7 | flower   light

sun _____

8 | drops   bow

rain _____

wh
ph

wheel   ele**ph**ant

Focus

Write the words with the pictures.

wheel	whisk	white	phone	photo
pheasant	alphabet	elephant	dolphin	

Key Words

when
where
which
while
what

wheel
whisk
white

phone
photo
pheasant

alphabet
elephant
dolphin

1 _____   2 _____   3 _____

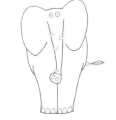

4 _____   5 _____   6 _____

7 _____   8 _____   9 _____

Finish these sentences with a word from the box.

> wheel   whistle   whisk   what
>
> white   where   whisper   whiskers

1 My mum uses a _____ when she makes a cake.

2 I painted the swan in my picture _____.

3 Tom and Isla always _____ to each other.

4 The _____ on my bike is broken.

5 The cat cleans her _____.

6 _____ are my shoes?

7 My teacher blew her _____.

8 _____ time is it?

un
beginnings

untidy

Focus

Write a key word to match each picture.

Key Words

undo
untidy
unlock
unfair
unlucky
unpack
undress
unzip
unload
unhappy

1 _____

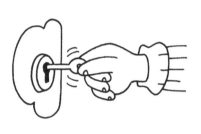

2 _____

3 _____

4 _____

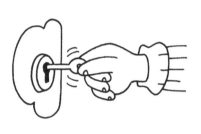

5 _____

6 _____

7 _____

8 _____

9 _____

Extra

Write the words next to the things you can see in the picture.

undo	undress	unhappy	unload
unlock	unlucky	unpack	unzip

a	b	c	d	e	f	g	h	i	j	k
l	m	n	o	p	q	r	s	t	u	
v	w	x	y	z						

Focus

alphabet

Write the alphabet in order using capital letters.

A

Key Words

letters

words

order

first

last

after

next

alphabet

Look carefully at these letters.

k   s   u   q   b   o   a   l   t

Use these letters to answer the questions about the alphabet.

1 Which letter comes at the beginning of the alphabet? _____

2 Which letter comes after j in the alphabet? _____

3 Which letter comes after a in the alphabet? _____

4 Which letter comes before t in the alphabet? _____

5 Write the vowel letters found in the box above. _____

6 Choose five of the letters.

_____   _____   _____   _____   _____

Write them in alphabetical order.

_____   _____   _____   _____   _____

Can you help the bee find its way back to the hive by colouring the units you've completed?

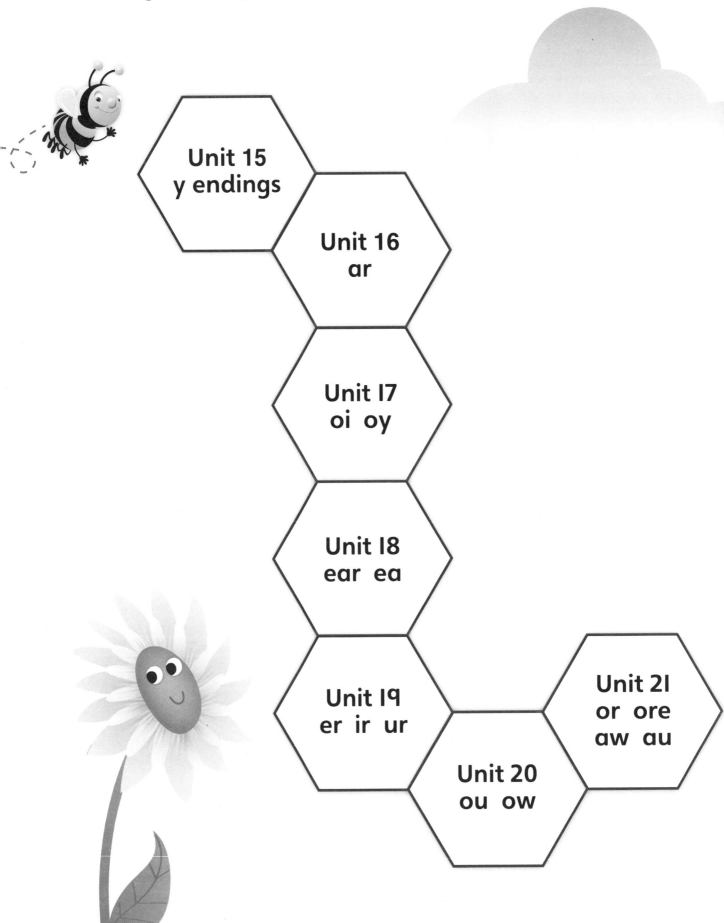

Unit 15
y endings

Unit 16
ar

Unit 17
oi oy

Unit 18
ear ea

Unit 19
er ir ur

Unit 20
ou ow

Unit 21
or ore
aw au